VIOLIN REPERTOIRE

NIIMI
VIOLIN SONG BOOK I
New Edition
Fingering and bowing by Yasuko OHTANI

新実徳英
ヴァイオリン・ソング・ブック I
新装版

大谷康子 運指・運弓

音楽之友社

ONGAKU NO TOMO EDITION

ヴァイオリン愛好家に贈る

プロ・アマを問わず、ヴァイオリンを愛好する人なら誰もが奏いてみたくなるような、そんな美しい、楽しいメロディ満載の曲集を作りたいと思いました。というのは、私自身、ヴァイオリンが大好きで、そのような曲集が欲しかったのです。《白いうた 青いうた》の旋律はそのためにうってつけの素材で、この歌集からヴァイオリン曲を作ることにしました。

1曲ずつ丹念に、まずアイディアを練り、そして奏いては書き、書いては奏きながら仕上げていきました。そうしないことには「ヴァイオリンの心」をつかむことができないと思ったからです。歌を作るとまず自分で歌ってみますね。それと同じことなのです。

そして、でき上がった曲を、また1曲ずつ、大谷康子さん (Vn) と私のピアノで演奏し、ボウイングをチェックし、指づかいを決めていきます。この最終段階での大谷さんのアドヴァイスはとても的確で、ヴァイオリンの技術的なことのみならず、音楽作りに至るまで、私は再三再四、蒙を啓かれる思いがしたものです。そしてなによりも、この初めて曲が音になる瞬間の楽しさ！

こんな風に作られた曲集を、私は全てのヴァイオリン愛好家に贈りたいと思います。1〜3の各巻共、そのままでステージが構成できる6曲でできていますが、使い方は全く自由。気が向いた時にどれか1曲をさらう、同好の友人たちと奏き合う、アンコールに1、2曲奏く、各巻からバラバラに数曲を選んで再構成する……等々、おおいにこの曲集を使って楽しんでいただければ、もって私の歓びとするところです。

（以上、初版時の序文）

＊＊＊＊＊

さて、このたび装い新たに計2巻の曲集として編まれることとなりました。今回も使い方は自由にしていただいて構いません。

また、《白いうた 青いうた》の元曲（2部版）、この『ヴァイオリン・ソング・ブック』、そして『ピアノ・ソング・ブック』を「往き来」しながらやる演奏会も楽しいものです。

時には小物打楽器などを加えても楽しいでしょう。いろいろな楽しみ方を発見していただけたら幸いに思います。

新実徳英

2017 年 9 月

TO VIOLIN LOVERS

I had long wanted to write a songbook full of pleasant melodies that lovers of the violin, whether professional or amateur, would feel like playing. I love the violin, and so I wanted such a book for myself. The melodies from "SONGS IN WHITE, SONGS IN BLUE" were the perfect materials for it and I decided to make a piece for violin out of the song collections.

In composing these melodies, I first developed them piece by piece with violin in hand, and as they gradually took shape I wrote them down. In the midst of this process, I played them again and again. How else, I thought, would I be able to grasp the essence of the violin through each melody. It was just like writing a song; one needs to sing it over and over in order for it to come to life. These violin melodies have come to life in the same way.

The next step in the process was to have them played piece by piece by an experienced professional. Yasuko Ohtani played them on the violin and I accompanied her on the piano. Together we checked the bowing and decided the fingering. At this last stage of composition, Ms. Ohtani's advice was exact and enlightening, not only in terms of violin technique but also for its musicality. And above all, I was filled with excitement and joy as each piece came to life in the hands of a true professional.

These three songbooks are the result and I would like to present them to violin lovers throughout the world. Each songbook contains six pieces which could be the equivalent of one longer piece in a full concert. But of course, you the player can use them as you wish. Practice one piece when you are so inclined; enjoy playing other pieces with your friends. Play one or two pieces as encores of a concert of entirely different pieces or reconstruct your own concert choosing pieces freely from the three books. It would give me pleasure if you discover other uses for these melodies, and in turn, I hope, this will give you even greater pleasure.

(The above is the preface of the first edition)

＊＊＊＊＊

In the meantime, these songbooks are to be re-edited into 2 volume collections with a new look. You are all welcome to any use of this version, too.

Also, I think it enjoyable to give a concert of which program goes back and forth among the works of the original song collections (2 part chorus version), this "VIOLIN SONG BOOK", and "PIANO SONG BOOK".

Adding small percussions or the like would probably be enjoyable on occasion. I am happy if you come to enjoy them in various ways.

Tokuhide NIIMI

September 2017, Tokyo

VIOLIN SONG BOOK 新装版

BIRDS SICILIANO 鳥のシシリアーノ	4
HABANERA IN WHITE 白のハバネラ	9
SPRING CHANSON 春のシャンソン	14
WALTZ IN THE RAIN 雨のワルツ	21
WIND TURNS 風まわる	28
BREEZE LULLABY そよかぜの子守歌	33
AUTUMN LEAVES DANCE 落葉の舞	38
A FISH STORY BLUES お魚のブルース	43
LA FOLIA IN BLACK 黒のラフォリア	48

Fingering & bowing by Yasuko OHTANI
運指・運弓　大谷康子

BIRDS SICILIANO
鳥のシシリアーノ

Tokuhide NIIMI
新実徳英

※ perfect fifth moved smoothly when the fingers are changed.
※ 指を変えると完全5度がなめらかにつながる

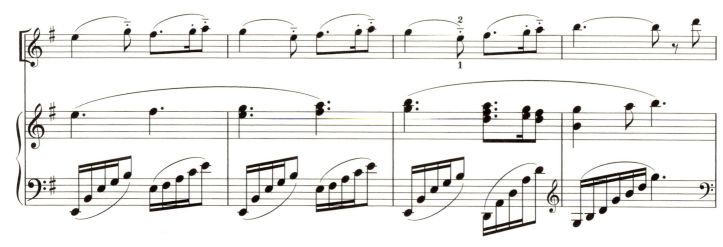

©2000 by ONGAKU NO TOMO SHA CORP., Tokyo, Japan.

HABANERA IN WHITE
白のハバネラ

Tokuhide NIIMI
新実徳英

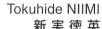

※ only when the lower notes of double
stopping are unable to be played,
the violin should be accompanied by the piano.

※：重音の下の音は省いても良い。但し、その場合は
　　┌─┐のPianoを奏すること。
　　下の運指は、上記が困難な場合、下記を用いること。

©2000 by ONGAKU NO TOMO SHA CORP., Tokyo, Japan.

SPRING CHANSON
春のシャンソン

Tokuhide NIIMI
新実徳英

©2000 by ONGAKU NO TOMO SHA CORP., Tokyo, Japan.

WALTZ IN THE RAIN
雨のワルツ

Tokuhide NIIMI
新実徳英

©2000 by ONGAKU NO TOMO SHA CORP., Tokyo, Japan.

WIND TURNS
風まわる

Tokuhide NIIMI
新実徳英

©2000 by ONGAKU NO TOMO SHA CORP., Tokyo, Japan.

VIOLIN
REPERTOIRE

NIIMI
VIOLIN SONG BOOK I
New Edition
Fingering and bowing by Yasuko OHTANI

新実徳英
ヴァイオリン・ソング・ブック I
新装版

大谷康子 運指・運弓

Violin

鳥のシシリアーノ *BIRDS SICILIANO* ——————— 2

白のハバネラ *HABANERA IN WHITE* ——————— 4

春のシャンソン *SPRING CHANSON* ——————— 6

雨のワルツ *WALTZ IN THE RAIN* ——————— 8

風まわる *WIND TURNS* ——————— 10

そよかぜの子守歌 *BREEZE LULLABY* ——————— 12

落葉の舞 *AUTUMN LEAVES DANCE* ——————— 14

お魚のブルース *A FISH STORY BLUES* ——————— 16

黒のラフォリア *LA FOLIA IN BLACK* ——————— 18

音楽之友社

BIRDS SICILIANO
鳥のシシリアーノ

Tokuhide NIIMI
新実徳英

※perfect fifth moved smoothly when the fingers are changed.
※指を変えると完全五度がなめらかにつながる

©2000 by ONGAKU NO TOMO SHA CORP., Tokyo, Japan.

SPRING CHANSON
春のシャンソン

Tokuhide NIIMI
新実徳英

WALTZ IN THE RAIN
雨のワルツ

Tokuhide NIIMI
新実徳英

©2000 by ONGAKU NO TOMO SHA CORP., Tokyo, Japan.

WIND TURNS
風まわる

Tokuhide NIIMI
新実徳英

©2000 by ONGAKU NO TOMO SHA CORP., Tokyo, Japan.

BREEZE LULLABY
そよかぜの子守歌

Tokuhide NIIMI
新実徳英

©2000 by ONGAKU NO TOMO SHA CORP., Tokyo, Japan.

AUTUMN LEAVES DANCE
落葉の舞

Tokuhide NIIMI
新実徳英

©2000 by ONGAKU NO TOMO SHA CORP., Tokyo, Japan.

A FISH STORY BLUES
お魚のブルース

Tokuhide NIIMI
新実徳英

LA FOLIA IN BLACK
黒のラフォリア

Tokuhide NIIMI
新実徳英

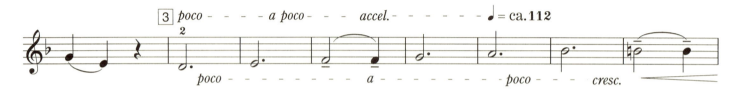

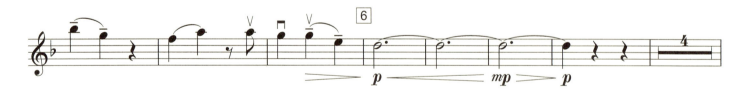

©2000 by ONGAKU NO TOMO SHA CORP., Tokyo, Japan.

BREEZE LULLABY
そよかぜの子守歌

Tokuhide NIIMI
新実徳英

©2000 by ONGAKU NO TOMO SHA CORP., Tokyo, Japan.

AUTUMN LEAVES DANCE
落葉の舞

Tokuhide NIIMI
新実徳英

©2000 by ONGAKU NO TOMO SHA CORP., Tokyo, Japan.

※ 1回目は上を，2回目は下を奏する。

A FISH STORY BLUES
お魚のブルース

Tokuhide NIIMI
新実徳英

※ gliss. of white keys

LA FOLIA IN BLACK
黒のラフォリア

Tokuhide NIIMI
新実徳英

©2000 by ONGAKU NO TOMO SHA CORP., Tokyo, Japan.

Tokuhide NIIMI

1947: Born in Nagoya, Japan
1970: Graduated from the Faculty of Technology at Tokyo National University
1975: Graduated from the Composition Class of the Tokyo National University of Fine Arts and Music
1977: Grand Prix of Composition at the 8th International Competition of Ballet Music, Geneva, and the Citizen's Award of Geneva.
1978: Completion of the post graduate course at the Tokyo National University of Fine Arts and Music
1982: Special Prize and Incentive Prize for Creative Stage Art at the Fine Arts Festival
1983: Member of the jury of the International Competition of Ballet Music in Geneva together with G. Petrassi, etc.
1984: Prize for Excellence at the Fine Arts Festival. Accepted at IMC.
2000: Awarded the 18th Nakajima Kenzo Prize.

He has contributed many remarkable works to the orchestral, chamber, piano and choral music repertoires. He is a present-day romantic, and one of considerable intelligence. His music reflects two worlds, the "melodic wind round" where all is delicacy, elegance and sensuality, and the "rhythmic wind round" which abounds with constructive, centrifugal energy. His recent creative activity is devoted to effecting a unification of these two worlds.

Remarkably, his orchestral works have been domestically performed by the NHK Symphony Orchestra and others, and in oversea countries they also have been performed by some of the leading orchestras, such as the Suisse Romande, Netherlands Radio, BBC Scottish, Radio France, Berlin, Nürunberg, etc.

新実徳英

1947 年　名古屋市に生まれる
1970 年　東京大学工学部機械工学科卒業
1975 年　東京藝術大学音楽学部作曲科卒業
1977 年　第 8 回ジュネーヴ国際バレエ音楽作曲コンクールにて史上二人目のグランプリ、ならびにジュネーヴ市賞を受賞
1978 年　東京藝術大学大学院研究科修了
1982 年　82 年度文化庁舞台芸術創作奨励賞ならびに特別賞を受賞
1983 年　83 年度ジュネーヴ国際バレエ音楽作曲コンクールの審査員を G. ベトラッシらと共に務める
1984 年　84 年度文化庁芸術祭優秀賞を受賞
　　　　IMC に入選する
2000 年　第 18 回中島健蔵音楽賞受賞

管弦楽作品ならびにピアノ作品や合唱作品を含む一連の室内楽作品は特に重要である。新実は、われわれの時代におけるロマンティストであり、同時に知的な存在でもある。繊細・優美、時に官能的な「線（旋律線）の纏りつき」を中心とした世界と、システマティックかつ遠心的エネルギーの噴出へと向かう「リズムの纏りつき」の世界、そしてその両者の統合へと創作の歩みを進めている。

管弦楽作品の多くは、国内では NHK 交響楽団をはじめとする主要オーケストラにより演奏されている他、海外ではこれまでにスイス・ロマンド、オランダ放送、BBC スコティッシュ、フランス国立放送、ベルリン、ニュルンベルグ等の各オーケストラにより演奏され、それぞれ高い評価を得ている。

VIOLIN SONG BOOK 新装版

菊倍版・ピアノ伴奏譜＋vnパート譜・各2400円

（ ）内は原曲タイトル

 I
- BIRDS SICILIANO　鳥のシシリアーノ（鳥舟）
- HABANERA IN WHITE　白のハバネラ（しらかば）
- SPRING CHANSON　春のシャンソン（二十歳）
- WALTZ IN THE RAIN　雨のワルツ（傘もなく）
- WIND TURNS　風まわる（夏のデッサン）
- BREEZE LULLABY　そよかぜの子守歌（北極星の子守歌）
- AUTUMN LEAVES DANCE　落葉の舞（落葉）
- A FISH STORY BLUES　お魚のブルース（ちいさな法螺）
- LA FOLIA IN BLACK　黒のラフォリア（中世風）

 II
- ROMANCE IN BLUE　青のロマンス（青い花）
- BURNING RED　燃える赤（ぶどうとかたばみ）
- LARK MARCH　ひばりマーチ（ぼくは雲雀）
- SPRING ELEGY　春のエレジー（春）
- IN THE SPRING　春に（春つめたや）
- WALTZ ON THE BEACH　なぎさのワルツ（なぎさ道）
- PAVANE FOR ROSES　ばらのパヴァーヌ（薔薇のゆくえ）
- AUTUMN RED　秋の紅（われもこう）
- GALLOP IN G　Gのギャロップ（自転車でにげる）

●初演の記録

「鳥のシシリアーノ」「白のハバネラ」
1998年8月20日　成増アクトホール
vn：大谷康子　pf：小山さゆり

「お魚のブルース」「黒のラフォリア」「落葉の舞」
1999年9月18日　けやきホール
vn：小松美穂　pf：石川裕司

「秋の紅」「なぎさのワルツ」「春のエレジー」
「ひばりマーチ」「そよかぜの子守歌」「春に」
2000年9月16日　けやきホール
vn：小松美穂　pf：須永真美

全曲
2001年3月31日　音楽の友ホール
vn：大谷康子　pf：榎本潤

First Performance

"BIRDS SICILIANO" "HABANERA IN WHITE"
Aug. 20th 1998, Narimasu Act Hall
vn: Yasuko OHTANI pf: Sayuri KOYAMA

"A FISH STORY BLUES" "LA FOLIA IN BLACK" "AUTUMN LEAVES DANCE"
Sept. 18th 1999, Keyaki Hall
vn: Miho KOMATSU pf: Hiroshi ISHIKAWA

"AUTUMN RED" "WALTZ ON THE BEACH" "SPRING ELEGY"
"LARK MARCH" "BREEZE LULLABY" "IN THE SPRING"
Sept. 16th 2000, Keyaki Hall
vn: Miho KOMATSU pf: Mami SUNAGA

Full-length Performance
March 31st 2001, Ongakunotomo Hall
vn: Yasuko OHTANI pf: Jun ENOMOTO

●CD

『ヴァイオリン・ソング・ブック』
カメラータ・トウキョウ　28CM-528
vn：大奥康子　pf：榎本潤

『VIOLIN SONG BOOK』
CAMERATA Tokyo 28CM-528
vn: Yasuko OHTANI pf: Jun ENOMOTO

ヴァイオリン・ソング・ブック I　新装版（しんそうばん）

2017年11月10日　第1刷発行

作曲者　新実徳英（にいみ とくひで）
運指・運弓　大谷康子（おおたに やすこ）
発行者　堀内久美雄

発行所　東京都新宿区神楽坂6の30
株式会社　音楽之友社
電話 03 (3235) 2111 (代)　〒162-8716
振替 00170-4-196250
http://www.ongakunotomo.co.jp/

476010

© 2017 by ONGAKU NO TOMO SHA CORP., Tokyo, Japan.
落丁本・乱丁本はお取り替えいたします。
Printed in Japan

本書の全部または一部のコピー、スキャン、デジタル化等の無断複製は著作権法上での例外を除き禁じられています。また、購入者以外の代行業者等、第三者による本書のスキャンやデジタル化は、たとえ個人や家庭内での利用であっても著作権法上認められておりません。

装丁：吉原順一
組版：福田美代子
印刷・製本：㈱平河工業社